MOZART

SELECTED INTERMEDIATE TO EARLY ADVANCED
PIANO SONATA MOVEMENTS

EDITED BY MAURICE HINSON

AN ALFRED MASTERWORK EDITION

Cover art: The English Tea at the House of the Prince of Conti
with Mozart Playing the Clavichord, *1776*
by Michel-Barthelemy Ollivier (1712–1784)
Giraudon / Art Resource, New York

WOLFGANG AMADEUS MOZART
Selected Intermediate to Early Advanced Piano Sonata Movements

Edited by Maurice Hinson

CONTENTS

This edition is dedicated to Dr. Melanie Foster Taylor, with admiration and appreciation.

Maurice Hinson

Foreword

Mozart's piano sonatas are staples in the pianist's repertoire and their popularity continues at an all-time high. This volume contains movements and some complete works that the advancing pianist can and should play. Von Nissen wrote in 1828:

At a time so rich in productive minds, when new works of music are constantly supplanted by still newer ones, it is surely worth taking the trouble to look at those works which will never suffer the fate of being pushed aside. Mozart's genius, which functioned in all areas of musical composition so felicitously as to erect in each a model such as his time had not seen—Mozart's genius crested, in piano music too, a marvelous cycle of works which, although infinitely diverse in nature, all bear the stamp of the highest perfection.[1]

Mozart composed fewer piano sonatas than Haydn or Beethoven. Each sonata is unique, yet together they form their own universe with emotional depth, humor and pathos. Their stylistic heritage is derived from Domenico Scarlatti, Carl Philipp Emanuel Bach, Johann Christian Bach and Joseph Haydn; they mix German, Italian and Viennese influences, and foreshadow Beethoven and Schubert. Mozart's dramatic intuition and emphasis on melodic line permeates them. "The way the hands behave makes the music similar to a dialogue; one constantly takes up the train of thought of the other, putting its case with still greater eloquence...."[2]

The circumstances surrounding the composition of many of the sonatas are unclear. In his early years Mozart did not notate his sonatas, but improvised them as required during his tours as a keyboard virtuoso. There were probably other movements and sonatas that were never written down. A few sonatas, once owned by Mozart's sister, have disappeared.

Mozart and the Piano Sonata

Mozart composed 19 solo piano sonatas, primarily between the years 1774 and 1778 when he was between 18 and 22 years old. He played some of these sonatas in public, but probably performed them more frequently in semiprivate surroundings to entertain members of his own family and their guests.

The form and scope of the piano sonata took on a new breadth with Mozart. This new purity of line and tender, nostalgic lyricism foreshadowed the *Sehnsucht* (longing) of the Romantics. He created some of his most lyric, profound and subtle moments in these terse and imaginative movements.

Pianists and teachers value the sonatas highly since they offer both musical and technical challenges. If they are to "flow like oil" (as Mozart was fond of saying they should), yet demonstrate a fine range of controlled dynamics, they require careful attention to detail, especially articulation.

The less advanced pianist often finds it easier to play some of the movements from Beethoven's piano sonatas, where the hand moves and shifts positions quickly, with its weight supported by the arm. Mozart keeps the fingers close to the keys for long passages, and requires quiet hands and a loose, flexible wrist.

How Mozart Played

The clavier (keyboard) completely dominated Mozart's whole career. He continued his career as a keyboard virtuoso throughout his entire life. It is possible to get some idea of Mozart's style of playing from his own words. First, there is his statement that "above all things a player should possess a quiet, steady hand, the natural lightness, smoothness and gliding rapidity of which is so developed that the passages flow like oil."[3]

Mozart regarded accuracy and precision highly, with every detail clearly presented, and his forte was evidently not in the nature of a violent contrast. The smoothness that he insisted upon so much resulted from evenness of touch on the Stein (his favorite) fortepiano, although it must have been acquired and equally evident on the harpsichord.

Mozart was particular regarding the position of the hand. It had to fall naturally and gently on the keyboard for full artistic expression. This quiet hand, connected so closely with the shal-

1. von Nissen, 147.
2. Ibid., 147.
3. Russell, 232.

low Viennese action fortepiano, was conducive to a meticulous clarity of detail.

The taste and expressive feeling that Mozart emphasized existed in his own playing. Haydn said: "I will never forget his clavier-playing as long as I live; it went directly to the heart."[4] Mozart's staccato, in particular, seems to have impressed everyone by its gracious brilliance and unique charm.

Mozart was a virtuoso, yet when he astounded his audiences with display, it was always perfectly balanced with feeling, taste and expression.

Mozart's letters contain a number of statements giving valuable information about the keyboard playing of others, and largely by inference, about his own style of playing. From a description of the playing of Nanette Stein, a child prodigy of Augsburg, Germany, written in a letter that Mozart wrote to his father on October 23, 1777, one learns that she sat quietly at the middle of the keyboard and played without making faces; that she kept the same tempo in repeated sections of a piece, although she probably varied it by adding ornaments and changing dynamics. One also learns that she kept the arm at keyboard level with a light wrist and the fingers continually in contact with the keys. Regarding tempo rubato, the left hand provided an accompaniment in strict time while the right hand played an independent and fluent *espressivo*, projecting the melodic line somewhat like a singer—much easier to describe than to perform!

Mozart notoriously disapproved of Muzio Clementi's brilliant and showy techniques. On January 12, 1782, he wrote: "Clementi plays well, so far as execution with the right hand goes. His greatest strength lies in his passages in thirds. Apart from this, he has not a *kreutzer's* [penny's] worth of taste or feeling."[5]

About his successful contemporary G. F. Richter, Mozart wrote on April 28, 1784: "He plays well so far as execution goes, but, as you will discover when you hear him, he is too rough and labored and entirely devoid of taste and feeling."[6]

From these criticisms, we are able to learn more about Mozart's approach to the keyboard. They also show something of his mental limitations, especially in regard to Clementi, whose advances in technique he failed to appreciate. Still, our exact knowledge of Mozart's playing is scanty. Accounts given by contemporaries are rather vague, and perhaps err on the side of adulation. It does seem that though he may have been surpassed in technique by some of his contemporaries, such as Kozeluch and Clementi, he stood alone in depth, feeling and imaginative power. There was, moreover, one aspect of Mozart's playing that earned him special renown, his prodigious improvisation. When his

imagination was excited, he and his instrument were as one. One of the most eloquent of many testimonies is found in Schlichtegroll's *Nekrolog* of 1793: "His whole countenance would change, his eyes became calm and collected; emotions spoke from every movement of his muscles, and was communicated by a sort of intuitive sympathy to his audience."[7] Mozart probably played many more notes when improvising than are found in the printed score.

The sociable Mozart was in constant demand to provide keyboard entertainment at informal and semiprivate gatherings. Michael Kelly, who sang in the first performance of *The Marriage of Figaro*, says:

> He favoured the company by performing fantasias and capriccios on the fortepiano. His feeling, the rapidity of his fingers, the great execution and strength of his left hand particularly, and the apparent inspiration of his modulations, astounded me.[8]

Mozart regularly performed keyboard duets with his sister, Maria Anna, called Nannerl by the family.

All accounts of his playing support the idea that Mozart brought his music to life by various means. These included singing tone, rhythmic verve, tasteful phrasing, clear differentiation between legato and detached notes, dynamic nuance, vital tempos and rubato in slow movements. These observations should be valuable to the pianist studying these sonatas today.

4. Broder, 43.
5. Ibid., 42–43.
6. Gerig, 55.
7. Schlichtegroll, 121.
8. Rosenblum, 23.

Performing Mozart's Piano Music

To perform Mozart's piano sonatas in a stylistic and historically informed manner, the pianist needs:

1. A smooth-flowing, clear and sparkling light touch. Light touch is especially important on modern pianos since they have a tone that is almost too big for Mozart's music.

2. A tone quality that is refined and cantabile (singing) in melodic passages.

3. A physical approach that is mainly finger and hand technique and avoids unnecessary movement and affectation. Mozart inherited a basic nonlegato style of playing from the harpsichord era. He does often demand a legato (with the appropriate slurs) for melodic passages, but his accompanying figurations should almost always be played nonlegato. Extended passages of triplets and 16ths should be played nonlegato. In Mozart's time most passages were not played legato unless specifically marked. Legato playing was the exception rather than the rule.

Written: *Played:*

4. An interpretation that includes moderation in tempo, rubato and dynamics, and elegant phrasing.

Technical Requirements

Technical requirements to play Mozart's piano works include the following:

1. Finger Action:

   a. Nonlegato touch: Distinct finger action is required. Keep the fingers as curved as possible for a nonlegato touch.

   b. Legato touch: Keep the fingers flat and stretched out. Finger pressure is required.

   Written:

   Played:

2. Scales and Arpeggios: Play these evenly and without bumps. Consequently, the wrist must be elastic and fast reactions in passing the thumb under are essential. Avoid the weak fourth and fifth fingers whenever possible. Thumb and fifth fingers may be used on black keys.

3. Trills: Trills should be even. In addition to the required finger movements, use the whole hand to trill, rotating from the elbow.

4. Octaves: Broken octaves are frequent in Mozart (see *Sonata in F Major*, K. 547a, Allegro, page 66, measures 45–49). Rotate octaves from the elbow while keeping the fingers in a fixed position.

Pedaling

The damper pedal should be used very sparingly with the movements in this collection. Mozart left no pedal indications, yet he was enthusiastic about the knee-pedal mechanism on the Stein fortepiano. In a letter to his father dated October 17, 1777, he wrote:

> The device which you work with your knee is better on his than on other instruments. I have only to touch it and it works; and when you shift your knee the slightest bit, you do not hear the least reverberation.[9]

Mozart probably made limited use of the damper-pedal mechanism of his day. In playing Mozart on the modern piano, pedal usage must be imperceptible. This requires very exact, shallow and frequent changes of pedal. Some of the fuller-sounding arpeggios or chords may be held with the fingers as long as the harmony doesn't change. This holding over was the original meaning of playing legatissimo. Articulation, clarity of texture and phrasing should never be obscured by the pedal.

The una corda (soft, or left) pedal should only be used when a definite change of tone quality is desired.

Ornamentation

Mozart's ornamentation was always distinguished and tasteful. Some of his embellishments are ambiguous, and for that reason ornaments are realized in this collection in footnotes. Three rules generally consistent with the practices of Mozart's day are:

1. Ornaments are played on the beat.

2. Trills normally begin on the upper note (the pitch above the written note).

3. Mozart's trills are usually written to end with a turn. A turn is usually played even when it is not written.

To perform all the ornaments that Mozart indicated is difficult even on old instruments (fortepianos). In difficult passages it is better to play the piece well without embellishments than to play it poorly with them. Each situation must be determined by the artistic conscience of the pianist.

Varied Repeats

In Mozart's day it was customary for the performer to vary repeats. Mozart probably never played any of his repeated sections the same way. In the foreword to his *Sonatas with Varied Repeats* (1760), C.P.E. Bach wrote: "Today varied repeats are indispensable, being expected of every performer."[10] Türk gives the following suggestions for varying repeats.

"Eight Basic Rules to be Followed by Performers When Varying Repeats" from Daniel Gottlob Türk's *School of Clavier Playing* (1789)

1. Ornaments must fit the piece; players are not allowed to show off.

2. Arbitrary embellishments must be as good as what is written. This means that it may often be best not to vary.

3. The same types of ornaments should not be used too often. Extensive additions should be left for the end of the piece.

4. Additions must appear easy.

5. Pieces expressing sadness, seriousness, simplicity, pride, majesty or solemnity should not be varied.

6. Tempo must be strictly observed.

7. Each variation must be based on written harmony.

8. The bass may be varied in keyboard music, but the harmony must stay the same.[11]

Türk further recommends that performers examine two vocal treatises, Pier Francesco Tosi's *Anleitung zur Singkunst* (1757) and Johann Hiller's *Anweisung zum Musikalisch—zierlichen Gesange* (1780). Both encourage elaborate improvisation, since the same ornaments in vocal music usually work well on the keyboard.

From later treatises, such as Johann Peter Milchmeyer's *Die Wahre Art das Pianoforte zu Spielen* (1797) and A. E. Müller's *Fortepiano-Schule* (1825), it is clear that the practice of improvised ornamentation, and particularly varied repeats, continued throughout Mozart's lifetime and into the early 19th century.

9. Ibid., 22.
10. Bach, 3.
11. Türk, 312–314.

Other Musical and Technical Considerations

A stylistic performance of Mozart's works requires a knowledge of the following musical and technical considerations:

Slurs

On the whole, Mozart's notation is rather complete regarding slurs. Even in the movements that have minimal dynamic markings, the slurs are always notated very carefully. Careful observance of the slurs is probably the single most important element in the proper interpretation of Mozart's music; using either the finger or the pedal to connect two notes that are separated by Mozart is the worst and most serious common fault in much Mozart playing.

Mozart used slurs to indicate:

1. Legato: A legato passage several measures long uses slurs that stop at the measure line, although in performance, no break between measures is intended.

2. Articulation: These short slurs are over two, three or four notes, and the final note is usually shortened.

Staccato Dots, Strokes and Wedge-Shaped Dashes

Mozart used the dot, the stroke and the wedge-shaped dash to indicate staccato. Since a quickly written dot and/or wedge-shaped dash can degenerate into a short stroke, it is often difficult to tell which was intended. For this reason, the editor has used only the dot to indicate staccato in this edition. When playing staccato notes, the pianist should always keep in mind the character of the piece, its tempo and the dynamics. If the character of the music is sad, serious or tender, staccato notes should not be as short as if it is cheerful or merry. Staccato notes in a singing adagio should not be played as short as in an allegro. In forte passages, staccato notes can generally be played shorter than in piano passages. Staccato notes are usually shorter in passages with leaps than in passages with adjacent notes.

Dynamics

Mozart used all the dynamic gradations between $\boldsymbol{pp}$ and $\boldsymbol{ff}$ ($\boldsymbol{pp}$, $\boldsymbol{p}$, $\boldsymbol{mp}$, $\boldsymbol{mf}$, $\boldsymbol{f}$, $\boldsymbol{ff}$), crescendo and diminuendo, but his use of $\boldsymbol{p}$ and $\boldsymbol{f}$ were used as merely basic types. The marking $\boldsymbol{p}$ can mean $\boldsymbol{p}$, $\boldsymbol{mp}$ or $\boldsymbol{pp}$, while $\boldsymbol{f}$ can mean $\boldsymbol{f}$, $\boldsymbol{mf}$ or $\boldsymbol{ff}$. The pianist must decide in each case which level to use.

About This Edition

Mozart: Selected Intermediate to Early Advanced Piano Sonata Movements is performance- and teaching-oriented and is based on the first Complete Edition, Brietkopf & Härtel, Leipzig, 1877–83. *The Neue Mozart-Ausgabe Bärenreiter-Verlag* (Kassel, 1986) was also consulted for textual differences.

Fingerings, metronome marks, pedal marks and indications in parentheses are editorial. Pedaling is a highly subjective matter, and any of the editor's pedal marks should be taken as only one person's suggestion. Either more or less pedal may be used than is indicated in some movements, depending on the instrument, room acoustics and other criteria that must be taken into consideration to achieve artistic pedaling. The pianist should experiment with half, quarter or very shallow pedaling as slow tempos and relatively slow harmonic rhythm invite some partial pedaling.

The editor's metronome marks indicate only the general or overall tempo of a given movement or section and must not be rigorously observed from measure to measure. Numerous ornaments have been realized in footnotes. History, performance problems and suggestions related to each sonata and sonata movement are discussed in "About the Music."

Understanding the form of each movement is vital to approaching a stylistic performance. This editor has always agreed with Robert Schumann, who said: "Only when the form is quite clear to you will the spirit become clear to you."[12] Therefore, the form of each movement is included and discussed.

These movements are not to be taught one after the other. According to the age and ability of the student, they should be interspersed with other Classical sonatas, with variations and with shorter Baroque, Romantic and Contemporary works.

Pieces are arranged chronologically and listed by their "K." numbers. The K. numbers refer to Köchel's *Chronologisch-thematisches Verzeichnis sämtlichen Tonwerke W. A. Mozarts* (Chronological, Thematic List of the Complete Works of W. A. Mozart). The first edition of this list was compiled by Ludwig von Köchel, and published in 1862. Subsequent revised versions (1937, 1947 and 1965) contained supplementary numbers and revisions. Where there were two numbers assigned, the latest appears in parentheses. The date listed under the title of each sonata is the date of com-

---

12. Schumann, 37.

position according to the *Neue Mozart-Ausgabe Bärenreiter-Verlag*, except for *Sonata in F Major*, K. 547a, which listing is from the *New Grove Dictionary of Music and Musicians* (1980).

Sources Consulted

Anderson, Emily. *Letters of Mozart and His Family.* 3 vols. London: Macmillan and Co., Ltd., 1938.

Bach, Carl Philipp Emanuel. *Sechs Sonaten für Clavier mit veränderten Reprisen.* Leipzig: J.G.I. Breitkopf, 1785.

Badura-Skoda, Eva, and Paul Badura-Skoda. *Interpreting Mozart on the Keyboard.* London: Barrie and Rockliff, 1962.

Broder, Nathan. "What Was Mozart's Playing Like?" *Etude* 9 (1956): 42–43, 64.

Einstein, Alfred. *Mozart: His Character, His Work.* London: Cassell, 1946.

Gerig, Reginald R. *Famous Pianists and Their Technique.* Manchester, NH: Robert B. Luce, 1974.

Maxwell, Carolyn, ed. *Mozart: Solo Piano Literature.* Boulder, CO: Maxwell Music Evaluation Books, 1987.

Neumann, Frederick. *Ornamentation and Improvisation in Mozart.* Princeton, NJ: Princeton University Press, 1986.

Nissen, Georg Nikolaus von. *Anhang zu Wolfgang Amadeus Mozarts Biographie.* Leipzig: Breitkopf & Härtel, 1828.

Rosenblum, Sandra P. *Performance Practice in Classic Piano Music.* Bloomington: Indiana University Press, 1988.

Russell, John F. "Mozart and the Pianoforte." *The Music Review* I (1940): 226–44.

Sadie, Stanley. *The New Grove Mozart.* New York: W. W. Norton & Co., 1980.

Schlichtegroll, Friedrich. "Johannes Chrysostomus Wolfgang Gottlieb Mozart." *Nekrolog auf das Jahr 1791.* Gotha: J. Perthes, 1793.

Schumann, Robert. *On Music and Musicians (1854).* Translated by Paul Rosenfeld. New York: W. W. Norton & Co., 1969.

Türk, Daniel Gottlob. *School of Clavier Playing (1769).* Translated by Raymond H. Haggh. Lincoln: University of

For Further Reading

Nebraska Press, 1982.

Bilson, Malcolm. "On Interpreting Mozart." *The New Hungarian Quarterly* Vol. XXX, No. 113 (Spring 1989): 212–220.

Marks, Helena F. *The Sonata: Its Meaning in Piano Sonatas by Mozart.* London: W. Reeves, 1921.

Rosen, Charles. *The Classical Style.* New York: W. W. Norton & Co., 1972.

Suggested Order of Study

(in increasing order of difficulty)

Sonata in E-flat Major, K. 282 (189g)

About the Music

This is the only Mozart sonata that begins with an Adagio movement (not just a slow introduction). The first and second movements reflect Italian influence in their expressive melodic quality. The concluding movement, an Allegro filled with Haydnesque rhythms and verve, has little stylistic similarity to the first two movements.

Form: Modified sonata-allegro (no development section). Exposition = measures 1–15 (first subject = 1–8; second subject = 9–15; codetta = 15); recapitulation = 16–33 (first subject [parts] = 16–26; second subject = 27–33; codetta = 33); coda = 34–36.

The opening three-measure melody serves as the main theme. A transitional ornamented theme follows through measure 8. At measure 9 the gracious but more complex second theme in the dominant appears and leads to the recapitulation at measure 16. Measures 16–26 utilize parts of the first subject and are full of contrasting dynamics and diminished harmonies. Measures 27–33 restate the elaborate second subject in the tonic. The first subject is used in the coda (measures 34–36) to bring this movement to an elegant close.

Menuetto I and II, which form the second movement, are an unusual combination of two minuets (usually called a minuet and trio) full of exquisite charm and simplicity.

Form: Ternary. **A** = measures 1–12; **B** = 12–18; **A**^{1} = 18–32. This courtly minuet contains graceful phrases in measures 1–12 only to be quickly contrasted with a short section of arpeggiated chords. The opening idea returns at measure 18 with the melody in the left hand.

Form: Ternary. **A** = measures 32–48; **B** = 48–56; **A**^{1} = 56–72. Menuetto II is longer and more involved than Menuetto I and contains strong dance rhythms punctuated with many dynamic changes. This movement may be considered the trio and concludes with a restatement of Menuetto I, without the repeats.

Form: Sonata-allegro. Exposition = measures 1–39 (first subject = 1–8; second subject **A** = 8–15; second subject **B** = 15–37; codetta = 37–39); development = 39–61; recapitulation = 61–102 (first subject = 61–69; second subject **A** = 69–76; second subject **B** = 76–100; codetta = 100–102).

This good-humored and sprightly movement provides a delightful conclusion to this sonata. The cheerful opening theme in measures 1–8 is followed by a second subject (part **A**), measures 8–15. The second subject (part **B**) is heard in measures 15–37 and leads to a codetta, measures 37–39. The rich development features modulating sequential ideas that lead to the recapitulation in measure 61.

Sonata in G Major, **K. 283 (189h)**

This delightful and popular sonata is the best-known of the six sonatas Mozart composed in Münich in 1775. The three movements of this sonata are well contrasted, with a stylish *galant* opener, a beautiful lyrical middle movement, and a puckish, delightful Presto finale with a brilliant conclusion.

Allegro **25**

Form: Sonata-allegro. Exposition = measures 1–54 (first subject = 1–16; transition = 16–22; second subject **A** = 23–31; second subject **B** = 31–43; codetta = 43–54); development = 55–72 contains only brief subtle suggestions of the exposition material; recapitulation = 72–121 (first subject = 72–84; transition = 84–90; second subject **A** = 91–99; second subject **B** = 99–111; codetta = 111–121).

This graceful minuetlike movement opens with a lyrical dialogue (question and answer) between the soprano and alto voices in the first theme (measures 1–4). The *fp* in measures 5–6 and 11–12 should be performed as small accents. Slightly more emphasis on these accents in measures 6 and 12 will lead naturally to the forte on the third beat and give added direction to the movement. Technical features include 16th-note scales and passagework, Alberti bass patterns, octaves, syncopation, parallel thirds, ornamentation played against moving notes, and two independent voices in one hand. The influence of J. C. Bach is seen in this movement in characteristics such as lightness, *buffo* character (fast enunciation of patter-texts originally in comic opera; here, fast articulated short notes as in measures 16–21), sweet melodies and a *galant* lyrical instrument style.

Andante **31**

Form: Sonata-allegro. Exposition = measures 1–15 (first subject = 1–4; transition = 5–8; second subject = 9–13); bridge = 13–15; development = 16–24; recapitulation = 25–39 (first subject = 25–28; transition = 29–32; second subject = 33–37); bridge = 37–39; coda = 39–41.

In the beautiful opening theme of measure 1, aim for intensity in the repeated Cs at the *p* dynamic level. The decrescendo in measure 7 is unexpected but beautiful. The second theme begins *f* in measure 9, in strong contrast to *p* of the first theme. The development (measures 16–24) focuses mainly on the first theme in various keys with embellished repetitions and an ascending chromatic passage in measure 24 leads to the recapitulation beginning in measure 25. The coda (measure 39 to the end) presents an elegant final look at the first subject.

Presto **35**

Form: Sonata-allegro. Exposition = measures 1–102 (first subject = 1–24; transition = 24–40; second subject **A** = 41–73; second subject **B** = 73–97; codetta = 97–102); development = 103–171; recapitulation = 172–273 (first subject = 172–195; transition = 195–211; second subject **A** = 212–244; second subject **B** = 244–268; codetta = 268–273); coda = 274–277.

This movement should not be played too fast. The exposition's second theme, beginning at measure 41, is gentle in contrast to the robust first theme. The development, which begins at measure 103, is one of the most dramatic in Mozart's early works due to its frequent modulations and sequential use of motives. Give full value to the measure rest (measure 171) that precedes the recapitulation. This movement contains subtle references to the other movements. The diminished harmony recalls the Andante, and the syncopated descending scales plus parallel voicing suggest the opening Allegro. This Presto movement is the most challenging of the early group of six sonatas and demands technical expertise and good dynamic control to make the dramatic contrasts effective.

Sonata in C Major, K. 330 (300h)

Form: Ternary. **A** = measures 1–20; **B** = 20–40 (**a** = 20–28; **b** = 28–36; **a** = 36–40); **A** = 40–60; coda = 60–64.

Einstein describes this expressive movement's character as "unclouded purity."[13] Its emotional intensity depends greatly on the use of the darker minor key in the middle section. The **A** section returns without repeat signs. Even though the autograph ends at measure 60, Mozart added the last four elegant measures when the sonata was engraved.

Sonata in A Major, K. 331 (300i)

Form: Ternary. Menuetto—**A** = measures 1–18; **B** = 19–30; **A**^{1} = 31–48. Trio—**A** = 49–64; **B** = 65–84; **A**^{1} = 85–101.

Since the minuet was the favorite dance of Paris, this work may have been influenced by Mozart's stay in Paris during 1777 to 1780. This simple and graceful movement is characteristic of Mozart's finest minuets. Mozart's quick shifts of emotion and clever manipulation of rhythmic structure transform the simple minuet into a compelling miniature of astonishing scope. The **A** section (measures 1–18) opens with a declamation and then moves into a lyrical theme accompanied by quiet Alberti bass patterns. This section dies away on the dominant at a piano dynamic level in measures 17–18. The short **B** section (measures 19–30) opens with a short three-note motif and moves sequentially toward a brief cadence in E major. Sequential motion in the **A**^{1} section (measures 31–48) follows, and 16ths lead stepwise to a tonic (A major) conclusion.

The serene D major Trio is also in ternary form, although the outer sections (measures 49–64 and 85–101) share only one brief measure of the exact same material (measures 49 and 85). Throughout, the left hand crosses repeatedly over right-hand thirds and sixths, a device reminiscent of Variation IV of the first movement. The inner section (measures 65–84) opens in a similar manner to the first theme outlining a dominant seventh chord to prepare for an octave passage in E minor. These octaves lead to a new C major melody (beginning in measure 73) that moves chromatically through several keys before returning to D major (measure 85) to end the Trio. The Menuetto is then repeated.

Form: Although this movement is often called the *Rondo alla Turca*, its form does not follow the generally accepted definition of a rondo. Its formal scheme consists of several small sections separated by double bar lines. Sectional: **I** = measures 1–24; **II** = 24–64; **III** = 64–88; **IV** = 88–97 (modification of measures 24–32); coda = 97–128.

Although written in a minor key (A minor), this movement is filled with playful humor and high spirits. It is one of Mozart's happiest and certainly best-known concluding movements.

Abrupt shifts from major to minor enhance the Turkish buffoonery. This work truly suggests a Turkish *Janissary* orchestra in miniature, and the piercing cry of the piccolo flute and the truculence of the kettledrums, cymbals, triangles and crescents are but a few of the orchestral effects. The fortepianos of the 18th century had numerous stops that could produce the sounds of bells, drums and kettledrums known as *Musique Turque*. The *Janissary* pedal, one of the best known of

---

13. Einstein, 245.

the early pedal devices, added various rattling noises to the normal timbre of the piano. It could ring bells, shake rattles, create the effect of a cymbal crash by striking several bass strings with a strip of brass foil, or even cause a drumstick to strike the underside of the soundboard.

This movement should be played as if it were merely a piano transcription of *Janissary* music! In the opening groups, played as four 16ths, the first note should be emphasized. The arpeggiated left-hand chords from measure 25 onward should be played just before the beat with great speed, so that the top notes in both hands occur simultaneously on the beat.

Janissary band. The "Turkish music" in works by Mozart, Gluck and other 18th-century composers was inspired by the sound of these bands.

Sonata in C Major, K. 545

This little gem, composed in Vienna on June 26, 1788, was written for young pianists. Although it is probably the most frequently played sonata of the Classical period, it was never published during Mozart's lifetime. This "Little Sonata for Beginners," as Mozart titled it, is clothed in unique simplicity yet tests the interpretive powers of the mature performer. Mozart, like Bach and Schumann, maintained the highest standards when writing for students.

Allegro **54**

Form: Sonata-allegro. Exposition = measures 1–28 (first subject = 1–12; second subject = 13–26; codetta = 26–28); development = 29–41; recapitulation = 42–73 (first subject = 42–57; second subject = 58–71; codetta = 71–73).

This short sonata-allegro movement is well balanced and uncomplicated. It is easy to play, but not easy to interpret. The opening should be played with great simplicity. Keep the Alberti bass figures quieter than the melodic lines while aiming for melodic clarity at all times. Finger-pedaling will add harmonic security to the movement if used carefully; the left-hand part in measure 1 would be played as follows:

Andante **58**

Form: Ternary. **A** = measures 1–32 (**a** = 1–8; a^1 = 9–16; **b** = 17–24; a^1 = 25–32); **B** = 33–48; **A** = 49–64 (**a** = 49–56; a^1 = 57–64; coda = 64–74).

The form of this serenadelike movement is simple, but the content is profound. The whole movement should be played with a dolce concept in mind, giving and taking slightly where emphasis is needed. The bass line in measures 41–48 should be projected to support the interesting harmonic development.

Rondo—Allegretto **62**

Form: Rondo. **A** = measures 1–8; **B** = 8–20; **A** = 20–28; **C** = 28–51; **A** = 52–60; coda = 60–73.

Strict imitation pervades this humorous and subtle short movement. Thematic ideas are short; two-note slurs plus parallel thirds add interest. Measure 51 should crescendo without ritard before the quarter rest.

Sonata in F Major, K. 547a

This sonata is not always included in complete editions of the piano sonatas since it is not certain that Mozart planned the movements to be performed together. The first movement is an arrangement from the *Piano and Violin Sonata*, K. 547, composed in Vienna in 1788. The keyboard arrangement may have been made at that same time. The sonata is usually printed with only two movements (Allegro and Allegretto), although it is possible that Mozart intended the theme and variations movement from K. 547 (arranged by Mozart for solo piano) to be a third movement.

Allegro **65**

Form: Sonata-allegro. Exposition = measures 1–78 (first subject = 1–16; transition = 16–31; second subject, part **I** = 32–64, part **II** = 64–78); development = 79–118; recapitulation = 119–196 (first subject = 119–134; transition = 134–149; second subject, part **I** = 150–182, part **II** = 182–196).

This charming movement opens with dramatic roulades moving around the F major tonic triad. Measures 16–31 present a transitional theme that moves to C major. The second subject (measures 32–78) includes a number of ideas featuring dotted patterns, broken chords, double thirds and scalar figurations. Technical challenges in the movement include facility with 16th-note passagework, divided and blocked chords, Alberti bass patterns, double thirds and sixths, broken and blocked octaves, repeated notes and ornamentation.

Rondo—Allegretto **73**

Form: Rondo. **A** = measures 1–8; **B** = 8–20; **A** = 20–28; **C** = 28–51; **A** = 52–60; coda = 60–75.

This movement is a transposition, with a few changes, of the third movement of the *Sonata in C Major*, K. 545 (see pages 62–64). The coda with its contrasting dynamics and dramatic ending is an improvement over that version, and for this reason Alfred Einstein believes the arrangement is definitely by Mozart.[14] The use of imitation in this movement is especially attractive. Dynamics should be well contrasted, especially those of the final four measures, where a surprise subito *f* ending follows the *pp* of measures 73–74. Various technical requirements include 16th-note Alberti bass patterns and passagework, double thirds, and two-note phrases.

---

14. Ibid., 252.

Sonata in B-flat Major, K. 570

This impressive late sonata was composed in February 1789, prior to Mozart's travels to the Prussian court to request a court appointment that had not been forthcoming nearer home. In this sonata, with its transparent sound, restrained gestures and profound spirit, Mozart makes ample use of counterpoint in a *galant* manner. Einstein called this sonata "perhaps the most completely rounded of them all, the ideal of his piano sonata—[it] also contains counterpoint used humorously in the finale as if in open reference to the secrets of which the work is full."[15]

Mozart in a silver-point drawing by Doris Stock in 1789, the year the Sonata in B-flat Major, K. 570 *was composed.*

Allegro **76**

Form: Sonata-allegro. Exposition = measures 1–79 (first subject = 1–20; transition = 21–40; second subject = 41–69 [note the opening of the second subject is the same as the first subject]; codetta = 70–79); development = 80–132; recapitulation = 133–209; (first subject = 133–152; transition = 153–170; second subject = 171–199; codetta = 200–209).

This movement, structurally one of Mozart's most compact, fluctuates in mood and feeling, but the final impression is one of quiet and gentle resignation. This sonata displays a wide variety of carefully marked phrasing and articulation. Short phrases are used in measures 1–4. Similar sections in measures 41–44 and 45–48 use long phrases. The longer phrasing is used in the development section while measures 133–136 in the recapitulation return to short phrases. This movement has no well-defined contrasting theme, but instead approaches the monothematicism of many Haydn sonatas. For example, the second theme heard at measures 41–69 begins like the opening theme. Thematic material occurs in both hands.

Adagio **86**

Form: Rondo. **A** = measures 1–12 (**a** = 1–4; **b** = 5–8; **a** = 9–12); **B** = 13–25; codetta = 25–28; **A** = 29–32 (first subject only); **C** = 33–40; codetta = 41–44; **A** = 45–48 (first subject only); coda = 49–56.

The first subject of this serene and profound movement is songlike and similar to the opening of the second movement of Beethoven's *Sonata in E-flat Major (Les Adieux)*, Op. 81a. Its first episode (measures 13–25) in C minor is closely related to the C minor passage in the middle movement of the Piano Concerto, K. 491. Measure 14 is almost literal quotation. The dialogue between hands in measures 25–27 is elegant when properly interpreted. The new theme at measure 33 requires a full, rich tone and must be projected over its broken-chord accompaniment. The coda is constructed with fragments of the various themes.

Allegretto **90**

Form: Ternary. **A** = measures 1–22 (**a** = 1–8; **b** = 8–14; **a** = 15–22); **B** = 22–62 (development of measure 3 of **A** = 22–42; transition = 42–44; development of new material = 45–62) **A** = 63–70; coda = 70–89.

The first subject of this cheerful and humorous movement illustrates Mozart's use of chromaticism. Chromatic and diatonic elements are juxtaposed so that measures 1 and 3 offer chromatic rises while measures 2 and 4 follow with diatonic descents. Measures 49–62 are excellent examples of Mozart's contrapuntal technique. Measure 89 is to be played *f*, but must be relative to the *p* dynamics of measures 85–88. The coda is based on parts of the development section. A charming simplicity permeates the entire movement.

---

15. Ibid., 249–50.

Sonata in E-flat Major

(1775)

K. 282 (189g)

Menuetto I

20

Menuetto II

Menuetto I D.C.

Sonata in G Major

(1775)

K. 283 (189h)

Sonata in C Major

(1783)

K. 330 (300h)

(f) From here to the end is missing in the autograph. However, Mozart added these measures when the sonata was engraved.

Sonata in A Major

(1783)

Menuetto

K. 331 (300i)

Trio

Menuetto D.C.

Alla Turca

ⓓ Later editions have F-sharp in place of the A.

Sonata in C Major

(1788)

K. 545

ⓐ Dynamics are editorial. ⓑ ⓒ

Andante (♩ = ca. 54)

ⓐ *mp (espressivo)*

p (legato)

cresc.

dim.

mp

p

cresc.

più f

ⓐ Dynamics are editorial.

Rondo

(a) The dynamics have been taken from the Allegretto movement of K. 547a (see pages 73–75),
which is a transposition of this movement.

Sonata in F Major

(1788)

K. 547a

Rondo

Allegretto (♩ = ca. 96)

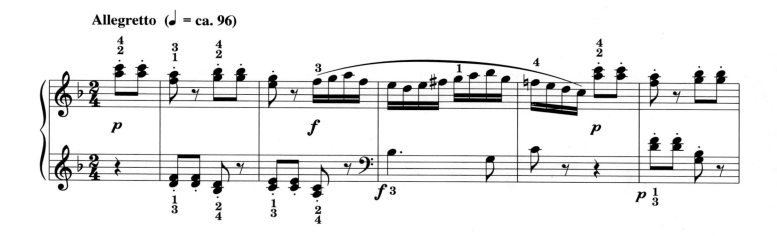

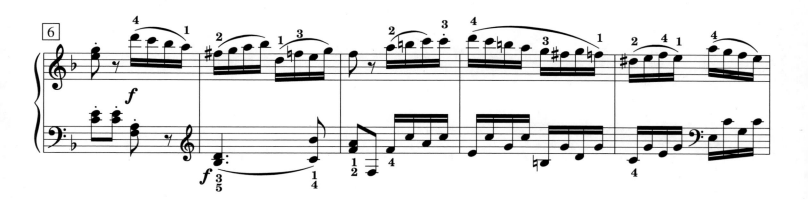

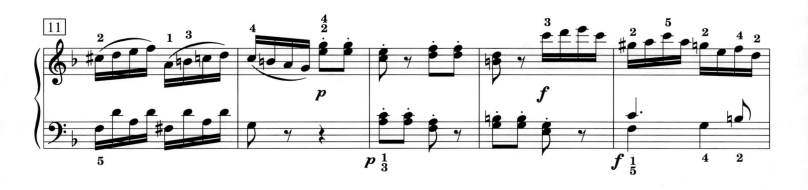

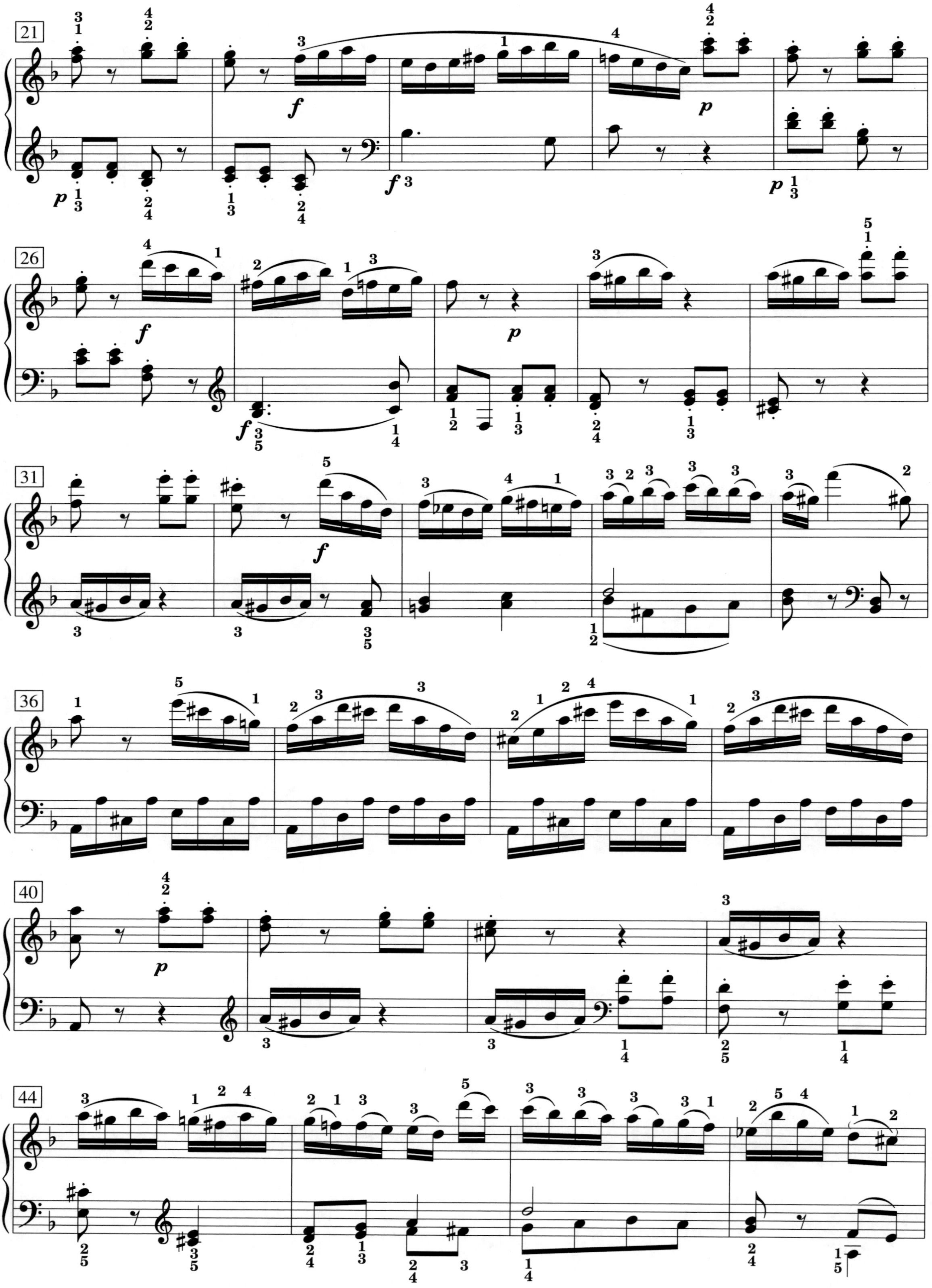
21
26
31
36
40
44

Sonata in B-flat Major
(1789)

ⓐ All dynamics in this movement are editorial.

Allegretto (♩ = ca. 69)

ⓐ All dynamics are editorial, except those in measures 82–89, which are from the first edition.

ⓑ

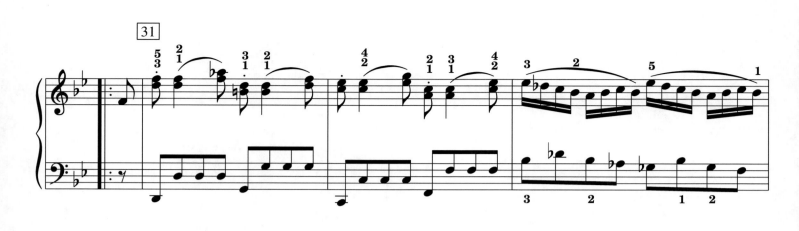